Shine Your Light:
A Kid's Guide to Reiki Healing
Teaching Companion

Shine Your Light:
A Kid's Guide to Reiki Healing
Teaching Companion

April D'Amato

Soul Star Healing

2019

To order this book, contact:
April D'Amato
april@soulstarhealing.com

Soul Star Healing
P.O. Box 1404
Guilford CT 06437

www.soulstarhealing.com

Dedication

To the New Children who have come to this planet to assist humanity with its great shift in human consciousness. They have come here to truly show us the way: to shed light on what is not working, to prompt us to make changes individually as well as globally, to challenge our beliefs and expectations, to defy our limitations and to expand our consciousness beyond duality and separation.

With the help of these children, we will embrace a new direction on Earth, one that includes peace, harmony and unity.

Table of Contents

Acknowledgements

I would like to thank the Archangels, my Spirit Guides and Galactic Team for helping me not only to create a class that embraces the sensitivities of these beautiful New Children to our planet, but also to write this book. I thank the Earth Angels, my friends, family and students of Reiki, for their love, support and faith in me.

I'd like to acknowledge my nieces Elesha D'Amato and Katie D'Amato for their invaluable presence in my life. Without realizing it, they have inspired me to work with children and write this book. Both Elesha and Katie have been attuned to Reiki energy healing from an early age; one attended one of my Reiki classes for kids and helped shape the curriculum for the Reiki kids' classes. They already have incredibly intuitive natures, and now, in Reiki, they have a tool that will last them a lifetime.

I thank Patricia Laudano for her plant wisdom and connection to nature spirits. Her words of knowledge encouraged the creation of the appendix on planting.

I thank Kate Clancy of Kelana Design, the masterful artist who not only created the cover of the book but also made the illustrations for the children's workbook that accompanies this teaching companion.

Finally, and most importantly, I extend a huge thank you to Susannah MacNeil for her endless patience, support and expert editing skills. Without Susannah, you would not be reading this right now.

Preface

Whether you call them indigo, rainbow or crystal children, the New Children have been arriving on our planet over the last 30 years to assist us with the great shift in human consciousness from separation to unity. When Whitney Houston recorded the song "The Greatest Love of All" in the 1980s, and sang "I believe the children are our future. Teach them well and let them lead the way," I doubt she or many others truly understood the significance of what was to come - and how very prophetic those words were. The new children truly *have* come here to show us the way: to shed light on what isn't working, to prompt us to make changes individually as well as globally, to challenge our beliefs and expectations, to defy our limitations and to expand our consciousness beyond duality and separation.

The New Children bring with them an evolved and markedly different human consciousness. The Earth and all her inhabitants are ready for this shift, and it has begun. The New Children are beacons of light from birth, sent forth by Spirit. Look closely at your children and you'll notice that they are, in fact, more precious than ever. They are born knowing who they are, why they are here and how they can change things; their gifts are astounding. Their light is steady and strong. They are ready to bring peace, balance and harmony to our planet. But they teach not through words but by their actions, behaviors and examples. They are here to test us, train us and lead us into a new consciousness by way of their sensitivities.

The New Children may seem to have difficulty fitting in. But is it really their problem or ours? One of the greatest tragedies I've seen is that we tend to want our child to "fit in" or conform, often because of our own issues with self-acceptance and belonging and our need for routine. These children, however, aren't meant to "fit in." They are highly sensitive human beings who ask us to change the way we think and do things. It's like trying to fit a square peg in a round hole. Our society tends to want to "shave" down the square pegs to fit when in fact it would make more sense to broaden the hole. But that would require changes in perception and behavior, which aren't always easy. So instead we tend to view the New Children 's sensitivities as weaknesses – and we miss a tremendous opportunity for them, for our society and for our planet.

It's no wonder that the New Children are often misunderstood. Because of their sensitivity, they experience resistance on every level – physical, mental, emotional and behavioral – and they are often labeled as having "problems." I believe their "problems" are similar to environmental allergies, but in their case they are allergic not only to physical things but also to the prevailing belief systems, attitudes and behaviors in families, communities and society as a whole.

Sadly, we as a society have become desensitized to many of the things that the New Children are here to change. We have allowed our inner voices to grow quiet. Look at the world today. There are so many factors that can impact the well-being of our children: food, healthcare, TV and the internet, and dysfunctional relationships to name a few. Every aspect of our world is begging for transformation, from how we grow and harvest our food to our damaged water supply, chemical contamination, violence toward ourselves and others, individual irresponsibility, and how we measure educational success. If the New Children are having difficulty with our way of life, maybe it's time for an overhaul.

I have a special passion for this topic because of my own experience. As a child, I was constantly physically ill, but there wasn't always a clear medical reason. That doesn't mean there was nothing wrong; it just means that doctors were missing the bigger picture. One of my intuitive gifts is that I'm an empath; that is, I can feel other people's "stuff." When I was young, I didn't realize that I was sensing other people's emotional energy and incorporating it into my own. I didn't have anyone to teach me how to handle the energy coming at me. Instead, I was overwhelmed by it and I got sick. (I believe the "illness" was actually more of an allergy to my environment.) This caused me a great deal of difficulty – so I learned to block my empathic skills and "fit in." Later in life, when I was ready to heal and explore myself more fully, I was able to reopen to my gift. Today, I and many others view my sensitivity as a blessing.

The New Children can have a very difficult time if they aren't treated with compassion and provided with guidance on their path. While they may not have completely forgotten why they are here, these children do tend to "shield" themselves – often in unhealthy ways because they don't know how else to do it. Asking them to "fit in" creates imbalance and/or dis-ease for them. The New Children often aren't capable of blocking out their gifts and they usually act out in some way, particularly through their behavior or by displaying developmental problems. If we take the time to pay attention, we'll discover that these children simply want to be heard and valued for who they truly are.

Since the gift of sensitivity has played a large role in my life, it has prompted me to help children learn how to use theirs. Teaching them to understand, navigate and use their energy/sensitivity is by far one of the favorite parts of my job. As these children grow into their full identities, it becomes quite a learning experience for everyone involved. We must shift our perception to understand that the changes the New Children seek will benefit all of humankind. Our Western medical approach usually consists of diagnosis, labeling and medication, perpetuating a consciousness of separation. If we allow the New Children to help us move into a consciousness of unity, we will realize that all living things are connected, and one thing impacts another.

There are many ways that you, too, can assist the new children on our planet:

1. Realize that children are not meant to "fit in." They are meant to stand out as the beautiful beacons of light that they are.
2. Remember that children need to be heard and validated. Listen to children and honor what they think, feel and say. How you respond to them will inevitably affect whether or not they believe in themselves.

3. Step for a bit into their world. Rather than making a judgment based on societal labels, allow them to show you who they are and what they experience through their perceptions of life on Earth.
4. Give them the tools they need to understand themselves and energy better. Seek out alternative forms of healing and care for them, and help them to learn those techniques for their well-being.
5. Teach children to tune in to, honor and respect their sensitivity. For I believe it is their sensitivity that will transform the people of the Earth and make way for the evolution of human consciousness.

The New Children need us to show them the way, by making room for *them* to show *us* the way.

Introduction

Reiki, an ancient Japanese energy healing technique, is the magic that we need to teach our children. Reiki energies flow automatically to where they are needed physically, emotionally, mentally, and spiritually to help heal the recipient. Reiki has limitless uses, and today it has advanced into the mainstream and become an acceptable healing modality used in hospitals.

Fortunately, Reiki is also not difficult for children to learn. When I first learned Reiki, I tried it on everyone I knew, including my four-year-old niece Elesha. She was having a terrible time trying to breathe because she had asthma. I asked Elesha if I could do some Reiki over her head and she said yes. She was so tired of feeling sick that she was willing to try anything. I stood behind where she was sitting and placed my hands a few inches over her head, not touching her; I asked if she felt anything. Elesha nodded yes. She told me she felt warmth. I wasn't surprised because I had heard this response consistently from others, but I didn't expect the description Elesha gave when I asked *where* she felt it. She said, "in my heart." Her answer brought tears of joy to my eyes. (As I mentioned above, I had only placed my hands over her head.) My four-year-old niece had captured the essence of Reiki healing so perfectly! Reiki is love. While adults question and sometimes struggle with the concept of Reiki, children understand it intuitively.

My experience with Elesha inspired me to work with children in a healing capacity. Compared with adults, most children are relatively unencumbered with life experiences, making them the ideal channel for Reiki energy. There are so many benefits to treating children with Reiki: improving concentration, enhancing sleep, and healing of physical, mental and emotional conditions.

There are many benefits to performing Reiki on children – but why not *teach* children Reiki? If I had known Reiki as a child, my life would have been different: less stressful and probably healthier too. Learning Reiki helps to keep children open as the natural energy channels they are. Reiki encourages empathy, a feeling of connection to *all* living things that children can carry forward into their human relationships. Reiki can also be instrumental in developing children's self-esteem. It provides a valuable tool to help them weather the stresses of growing up. Reiki energy healing encourages self-awareness and self-empowerment. As a student of Reiki yourself, you know the healing and life-changing experiences that are possible. Unlike adults, children have fewer blocks to work through, so practicing Reiki gives them a forum for manifesting lives of love, peace and harmony. Why make our children wait to discover the magnificence of Reiki? Imagine the gift we can give them! See Appendix A for more about the benefits of children learning Reiki.

When I began teaching Reiki to children, I didn't have any materials to teach from. In preparation for every class, I would write some notes and create handouts for the children. I literally rewrote the book with every class. After my initial classes, I started to see a pattern develop. The children in my classes needed more than just Reiki. They all seemed to have a few things in common: they were bright, sensitive beings, but they seemed to experience a form of anxiety, an inability to express themselves and difficulty interacting with each other. I realized that they needed not only Reiki instruction but also direction to help them to connect with others, use their intuition and understand their feelings. They needed to discover themselves and learn to shine their light for the world.

I finally decided to create a workbook I could share with the children in my class, and over three years I created the complementary volume to the book you are now reading. This companion manual is designed to provide you with suggestions and exercises to teach a Reiki class to children as they follow along using the workbook. The student workbook itself has several beneficial exercises and questions that you can incorporate into your classes, but I felt that you may need further guidance. So I created this teaching manual with three parts – Planning Basics, Activities, and Reiki Instruction – as well as a generous selection of additional resources in the Appendices.

While this manual presents some general guidelines for teaching Reiki to children, it is meant to augment, not replace, your prior experience teaching Reiki to adults. All of the ideas you'll find here are ones that I have either successfully used myself or learned from other Reiki professionals. In general, the key to being a good teacher is to allow your intuition to flow through you as your guide. But to be an even better teacher with children you'll need to be as authentic with them as possible. In other words, don't just "talk the talk;" actually "walk the walk."

Planning Basics

Congratulations on making the decision to teach Reiki to children! When you bring together the openness and wonderment of a child with the energy of Reiki healing, you create the opportunity for magic here on Earth. Your Reiki class will help children develop skills that will take them forward into their adult lives as well as putting them in touch with the subtle energy and teaching simple methods of healing. Children are teachers, guides and future leaders – and teaching them Reiki helps them gain clarity and validates their inherent abilities as healers. You will learn from them as much as you will teach them, if not more.

The goal for the class is for children to leave with a greater feeling of self-confidence, empowerment and the ability to use Reiki in their lives. It's critically important that you create a nurturing, supportive environment in your classroom so that your students can discover their potential not only as energy healers but also as highly intuitive beings. The class is designed to be fun and interactive, with a child's well-being in mind, and it should be fun for you too!

In this section, I've gathered some thoughts on where to begin once you decide you want to hold a children's Reiki class. Planning your class is a lot easier than you think, but there are some guidelines to follow that will make it even easier. Please see Appendix B for a Sample Class Registration Form.

8 Things to Consider as You Plan Your Class

1. **Age Groups:** Break your classes down into age-appropriate groups. This book is ideal for working with young children to early teens. I like to divide up the age groups as follows, but I maintain some flexibility depending on the ages of the children who are interested. Use your judgment when considering whether a particular older or younger student would be an appropriate addition to the class.

   a. Ages 5 to 6
   b. Ages 7 to 9
   c. Ages 10 to 13
   d. Ages: 14 to 15

2. **Class Location:** Look for a place that is safe and ready for children. The classroom space should be large enough for your students to move around comfortably. Access to the outdoors is essential: It provides ample space to perform some of the exercises in good weather and it also allows children to connect more fully with nature.

3. **Class Length:** Consider the age group when deciding how many sessions you will offer and how long they will be. Younger children will have a shorter attention span. I take great care to schedule classes at a time when my own energy level is optimal, because when working with children you really want to be alert and quick. Below are some suggestions for how I set up my classes. Please see Appendix C for a sample Children's Reiki Class Outline.

   a. 1 hour a week for 8 to 10 weeks
   b. 2 hours a week for 4 to 5 weeks
   c. 3 hours a week for 3 to 4 weeks
   d. 4 hours a week for 2 to 3 weeks

4. **Healthy Snacks:** Offering a healthy snack during your class not only reinforces healthy food choices, it also provides a nice opportunity for socializing and helps children ground their energy. The timing of the snack is best determined based on the length of the class, so it will vary. For longer classes, I recommend timing the snack as a break; it gives children the opportunity to unwind a bit from paying attention. For shorter classes, I like to offer a snack at the end of class to help children ground. If your schedule allows and you're comfortable with the idea, you can use snack time to show students how to make their own quick, easy, healthy snack. Do be careful of food allergies, though; they are on the rise and sensitive children are most often affected. You'll find some sample snack recipes in Appendix D.

5. **Class Size:** Class size will depend on the age group you are teaching and whether you are teaching alone. If no one is assisting you in class, then you should have no more than four children in class at a time. Try to keep the class an even number of students so that no children feel left out. If you need assistance, ask whether any of the parents want to volunteer to help; if they do, you may want to offer them a discount on the class price. The younger the children, the more helpful it is to have volunteers to assist you.

6. **Class Schedule:** Be flexible when planning what will happen in a given class session. Even the best laid plans don't always go as we would like – and that's especially true with children. It's important to have a few activities in mind as backups in case your original plan isn't working. After you've taught a few sessions, your intuition will kick in and you will discover what works and what doesn't.

7. **Movement:** Children need an outlet for movement. You can include some stretching for energy balance, mindful movement, yoga postures or simply include some danceable music. Stretching is a very necessary component of energy work. You will find some sample movements in Appendix E.

8. Class Rules: These should be established during the first class together with the children and posted in a place that is visible for everyone to see for the remainder of the classes. Ask the children to help you decide what rules are important to have, their participation here is essential, it helps determine how they will conduct themselves in your class. Depending on the age group you are working with you, you may need to start off with suggestions for them. An example of a rule is: use kind words when speaking. Review these rules at the beginning of each class, and remember you can always add to them.

Activities

This is the fun section of the book! I've listed activities by category to match the different sections in the student workbook. This will make it easier for you to find and select activities when preparing for your class. Be sure to consider your age group when selecting an activity; some of the exercises below can easily be adapted for different age groups while others cannot. Once you begin teaching you'll develop a good sense of how long each activity will take based on the particular student group and your own teaching style. The suggestions below are proven techniques, but you are absolutely welcome to incorporate your own ideas.

Ice Breakers/Socialization/Connection

These activities will help you and the children begin to engage with one another. Some children are extremely shy and uncomfortable in group settings; a little relationship building will help put them at ease. The more comfortable the children are, the more participatory the class will be. I suggest choosing an exercise and spending about 15 minutes with it. However, this is where you will want to use your discernment in determining if an exercise needs more or less time.

1. **Common Ground**
   Supplies Needed: Paper, pens
   Instructions: Have the children come together in pairs and give them a specific amount of time (perhaps 5 minutes) to write a list of everything they find they have in common with the child they are paired up with. When the time is up, have the children share what they learned from one another about what they have in common.
   Alternate Instructions: To adapt this for a younger group, you can prepare five *"starter"* questions for the children to ask each other. The questions can be simple, such as *What is your favorite color? What is your favorite season? What is your favorite food?* etc. Print the list before class begins so the children can answer those questions first. After they are done asking questions, they can compare notes with each other to find out which answers they have in common and then share their discoveries with the group.

2. **Find Someone Like Me**
   Supplies Needed: Paper, pens, pictures
   Instructions: Provide several identical cut-outs of items such as animals, colors, trees, sports teams, etc. Ask each child to select picture(s) of the things they like. Then have the children walk around the room to find other children with the same picture(s). Have them discover how many of the other children have the same interests and then share their findings with the class. This is an easy activity for a younger age group.

3. **Pass the Ball**
   Supplies Needed: A small, soft ball
   Instructions: Have the children sit in a circle and roll the ball to each other. When each child receives the ball, they will tell you something about themselves. You can repeat this exercise at the beginning of a later class to reinforce what they've learned in a previous class.
   Alternate Instructions: To adapt for older children, ask the children to stand in a circle and have them toss the ball to each other instead of rolling it.

4. **Guess the Animal**
   Supplies Needed: Pictures of animals, tape
   Instructions: Have the children line up in two rows with their backs to one another. Tape a picture of an animal to each child's back. Do not let them see what animal it is. The goal is to have each child identify the animal on their own back by asking other children for help. Only "yes" and "no" questions are allowed. Once a child guesses their animal, they can remove the picture and place it in front of them. You may need to encourage the children to keep helping each other once they have discovered their own animal. A tip: When choosing the animal pictures for this activity, make sure the animals are ones that your particular age group will be able to identify.

5. **Beach Ball Toss**
   Supplies Needed: One beach ball, permanent markers
   Instructions: Write phrases all over the beach ball such as *favorite food, favorite color, birthday month, most embarrassing*, etc. Have the students stand in a circle and pass the beach ball around the circle by throwing it up in the air. When the ball is in the air, the person who just threw it should call out the name of a finger (thumb, index finger, etc.). The person who catches the ball must read and answer the question under or nearest to the corresponding finger.

6. **Music, Instruments & Free Dance**
   Supplies Needed: Toy instruments, recorded music
   Instructions: Play music that is upbeat and danceable and that encourages movement. The first time you introduce this exercise, allow a good 15 to 20 minutes for the children to relax into it. This activity is one you'll want to join in; your participation will help them feel more comfortable expressing themselves. I keep a variety of instruments on hand, such as rattles, tambourines, drums and bells. This exercise is a great way to start each class because it helps the kids get grounded and refocused and it clears out any chaotic energy they may have brought with them (for example, if they rushed to class, had an argument, or are feeling sad). If dancing is not your thing, check out Appendix E for Yoga/Mindful Movement suggestions. You'll find music suggestions in Appendix F.
   Alternate Instructions: To adapt this for older children, after the first time you do this exercise, encourage the children to bring in music they enjoy. It's okay to expose the children to different music, but it would empower them to share their music with you too.

Energy Exercises

Most children have learned the dictionary definition of *energy*. These activities are intended to introduce children to the concept of energy with regard to *energy healing*. The activities in this section will give your students the opportunity to sense energy through their hands and eyes.

1. **Creating the Energy Ball Together**
    Supplies Needed: None
    Instructions: You'll find a picture of an energy ball in the *Shine Your Light* workbook. When you have completed creating the energy ball, ask each child to place "their ball" into a part of their body such as their heart, leg, tummy, etc. Ask them to explain what they sense when they do this.

2. **Pass the Energy Ball Around**
    Supplies Needed: None
    Instructions: Gather in a circle or pair off to create an energy ball and pass it around. Each person should add their energy to it, which will make the ball grow. As the ball is passed, ask the children to feel and fully experience the ball growing larger and heavier, or even lighter. They can even reshape the ball as it if were modeling clay. When you are finished with this exercise, have the children place the ball into the Earth to help heal the Earth.

3. **Create a Pendulum**
    Supplies Needed: Thread, buttons, beads or crystals, fishing wire.
    Instructions: This activity is best reserved for older children. You'll need a weighted item on one end to create the pendulum; what kind of item is up to you. You'll find a picture of a pendulum in the *Shine Your Light* workbook. Once the pendulums are finished, have each child hold a pendulum over their palm and watch how it moves. Each child's "pendulum circle" may appear different; some may be circular or elliptical. This can become a great tool for them to detect energy and a visual expression of energy movement. Spend a few extra minutes to show children how to use the pendulum for "yes" or "no" questions.
    Alternate Instructions: To adapt this for younger children, you can provide them with a pre-made pendulum they can practice with and take home.

4. **Feel Each Other's Energy I**
    Supplies Needed: None
    Instructions: Pair the children up standing or sitting and facing each other. Ask them to hold their palms facing out, about 12 inches from each other. Encourage them to sense their partner's energy and describe it. Tell them to move backward until they can't sense their partner's energy anymore.

Aura Exercises

The activities in this section are intended to expand upon the energy knowledge gathered in the previous section. You can use them after teaching about auras – they're a great way for children to experience auras by interacting with other children in the class.

1. **Arms Wide**
    Supplies Needed: None
    Instructions: Ask the children to stand up and stretch their arms out wide by their sides. Then have them walk around the room trying not to walk into each other. Call out directions, for example, *Turn left now, Walk backward now, Take three steps forward,* etc. This will show the children how easily they come into contact with others' auras and how frequently they interact with one another without realizing it. This exercise will make the best sense if you do it *after* you have explained about the aura.

2. **Feel Each Other's Energy II**
    Supplies Needed: None
    Instructions: Similar to "Feel Each Other's Energy I," ask the children to stand across from each other a few feet apart, with their hands almost touching. Have them move backward so that each child is at least 12 feet apart from their partner. Ask the first child in each pair to turn around, while the second child continues to face the same direction. Have the second child put their hands up in a pushing direction. Ask the first child to let you know whether they feel anything. The second child may need to move closer until the first child can feel them. Then ask the second child to turn around, and ask the first child to face the second child's back. Ask the first child to make a push-pull movement to see if they can sense the other child's energy.

3. **My Aura**
    Supplies Needed: Giant roll of paper, crayons or colored pencils, markers
    Instructions: This exercise is best reserved for younger children due to their height, but children of all ages enjoy it. If you have 6 or more students, you may want to break them up into groups to do this exercise. Roll out the paper on the ground, and have one child lie down on the paper while the other children trace the outline of the child lying down. When they are done tracing, have the child stand up in front of a white wall and ask the other children to describe what they see: it could be around their aura, in their aura, on their body, etc. After the children begin to see things, have them draw what they saw and where they saw it on the picture that was just traced. You will be amazed by what these children can see—they see so much around each other. (They see a lot more than adults do!) Each child gets a turn. When they are done with the pictures, discuss what they discovered; they may have had non-visual experiences too.

Chakra Exercises

The activities in this section use sound predominantly to teach the children about their Chakras. The children tend to love these because they are given permission to make a lot of noise.

1. **Sound Test**
   Supplies Needed: Rattles, bells, drums
   Instructions: These items are used to detect changes in the "sound" of energy. This is a very subtle energy exercise, but it can be heard relatively well as long as the children are quiet and focused. The teacher would show the students how to play the instrument in front of each chakra, starting at the top chakra and working your way down. For instance, if you are using a rattle, shake the rattle consistently on the way down to see if you can sense the subtle sound changes as the rattle moves over each chakra.

2. **Chakra Toning**
   Supplies Needed: None
   Instructions: There are sounds associated with each chakra. Not only is this a fun exercise for children, but it's also great at clearing, opening and activating the chakras. To perform this exercise, instruct the children to take a deep breath in and exhale one of the sounds below for as long as they can. Once you teach the sounds, you can play with them a bit. For example, you can tone the sound "Oh" like a siren—going all the way up and all the way down.

   Root Chakra: "Uhhh" (as in *ugh* after a long day)
   Sacral Chakra: "Ooo" (as in *ooo la la*)
   Solar Plexus Chakra: "Oh" (like a powerful *no*)
   Heart Chakra: "Ah" (as in *ahhhh*)
   Throat Chakra: "I" (as in *eye*)
   Third Eye Chakra: "A" (as in the name *April*)
   Crown Chakra: "E" (as in *eek*)

3. **Chakra Discussion**
   Supplies Needed: *Shine Your Light* workbook
   Instructions: There are questions in the workbook that will really be helpful for class discussion. The children can take them home and bring them in for discussion during the next class, or you can go through the questions out loud as a group.

Exercises for the Senses

The activities in this section introduce the children to their sixth sense, better known as their intuition. This will encourage them to explore experiences they have already had or inspire them to want to learn more.

1. **Nature Walk**
   Supplies Needed: A nice spot outdoors
   Instructions: If you have access to a nice area outdoors, take the kids out for a stroll. Have the children walk up to flowers and trees and try to sense their auras.

2. **Meet Your Angels, Spirit Guides, Animal Totems or Fairies**
   Supplies Needed: Written guided meditation, or improvise your own
   Instructions: You can write your own guided meditation for the children to meet the helpful spirits around them: angels, fairies or animals. This should be a short exercise; use your judgment to decide whether it's a good one for your particular group.
   Alternate Instructions: Briefly teach the children about the most common Archangels that they can easily access for their own protection, for healing work and for whatever else they may need assistance with. The Archangels are Raphael, Michael, Gabriel and Uriel. See Appendix G for an easy prayer the children can say before bed and/or before doing Reiki.

3. **Pinwheel Breathing**
   Supplies Needed: Handheld pinwheel
   Instructions: Practice breathing with a pinwheel toy. This exercise teaches children to quiet their minds and focus on their breathing. Have each child hold their own pinwheel in their hand, and ask them to inhale a deep breath and then exhale that breath fully to make the pinwheel turn. The exercise can also be performed with a balloon.

4. **What Do You See**
   Supplies Needed: Paper, pencils or pens
   Instructions: This game teaches children to be in the present moment so that they can notice their intuition. Ask the children to look around the room and try to remember everything they see. Then have them close their eyes, take three deep breaths, and then write down everything they saw.
   Alternate Instructions: To adapt this for younger children, eliminate the writing portion: Simply have them keep their eyes open, look around the room and name everything they see. It brings them into the present moment. Then have them close their eyes and try to remember what they saw.

5. **Dream Talk**
   Supplies Needed: Group Discussion
   Instructions: Talk about any dreams or intuitive experiences the children might have had. You can suggest that, before they go to sleep, they ask the angels to help them remember their dreams in the morning. Tell them to keep a notebook by their bed and write down their first thoughts – or even entire dreams, if they want to. Explain that keeping track of dreams helps us notice common themes and intuitive messages.

6. **Grounding**
   Supplies Needed: A nice outdoor space (optional), written guided meditation
   Instructions: You can find a variety of grounding activities in the companion *Shine Your Light* workbook. Grounding is a great exercise to do with children outside; it's a great opportunity to lead a guided meditation to connect them to the Earth. Explain to them that the roots or cord of light that you are sending into the Earth are like the roots of a tree. Please see Appendix H for information on how to purchase a recorded Children's Grounding Meditation.

7. **Fairy Dust Adventure**
   Supplies Needed: Birdseed, edible glitter, dried flower petals, cornmeal, mesh pouches, plastic or metal spoons, bowls, a nice outdoor space with trees, guided meditation
   Instructions: Place the ingredients in separate bowls. Tell the children a story about how the fairies reside in nature, and love to interact with children, but they often hide from sight unless they know it is safe and they are welcomed. Explain to them that making the fairy dust and placing it outside near a tree lets the fairies know that someone is open to see them and interacting with them. Give each child a mesh pouch, or a paper or plastic sandwich bag, along with a small bowl and spoon. Ask each child to scoop a little of each ingredient into their bowls and mix them together before pouring it into their pouches. Remind them not to forget the glitter, because fairies love sparkles. (I use edible glitter because it is safe and biodegradable.) Guide the children on a meditative, conscious walk to find the perfect tree where they can sit and sprinkle some fairy dust at the base of the tree. Have them sit quietly and envision fairies through a guided meditation or discussion.

8. **Oracle Cards**
   Supplies Needed: *Magical Unicorns Oracle Deck* or *Magical Messages from the Fairies* by Doreen Virtue.
   Instructions: These oracle cards are kid friendly with messages like play more, love yourself, etc. Guide the children to close their eyes and focus on their breath. Tell them to think about something that is bothersome to them or something they want. After they have thought about what they want or what bothers them, ask them to pick a card and that is their message from the unicorns or fairies depending on the deck you choose. Another way to use this deck is to have them pick a card and discuss their feelings around what the card is saying to them.

Exercises for the Feelings

These activities are intended to explore feelings and emotions, particularly the ones expressed in the companion workbook. The best time to do these exercises is after you have established a relationship with the children so that they will feel more comfortable. Please see Appendix I for Additional Resources that will help you to introduce the topic of feelings.

1. **Feelings Rainbow I**
   Supplies Needed: *Shine Your Light* workbook
   Instructions: Talk about the different feelings people experience and the colors associated with them. E.g, "She feels blue" means she feels sad; "he sees red" means he is angry. Have the children create their own rainbow of emotion in their workbooks.

2. **Feelings Rainbow II**
   Supplies Needed: Paper (colored or plain), colored sticky notes, markers, tape
   Instructions: Create a large rainbow with each color representing a feeling (happy, angry, sad, etc.). Tape it to the wall. Assign a feeling or emotion to each color in the rainbow. At the beginning of each class, ask the children to take a sticky note that's the "color" they are feeling and have them place it on the rainbow. The sticky notes from each class will continue to accumulate on this rainbow so they can see their feelings over time.
   Alternate Instructions: To adapt this exercise for younger children, create pre-cut "smiley face" pictures that express different emotions. Ask each child to post a picture on that matches their feelings the large rainbow.

3. **Map My Feelings on My Body**
   Supplies Needed: Outlined pictures of a body similar to one in the *Shine Your Light* workbook; crayons or pencils
   Instructions: Give each child a body outline and ask them to them identify the body parts where they feel certain feelings. Have them write the name of the feeling on the corresponding body part.

4. **Fishing for Feelings**
   Supplies Needed: Box or jar, markers, colored paper; Velcro tape and toy fishing pole (optional)
   Instructions: Cut fish shapes out of paper and write a different feeling on each fish corresponding to a feeling discussed in the workbook. Decorate a box or a jar to look like a fishbowl, and place all the paper fish inside. Ask each child to pull out a fish. (For a more challenging exercise, use a toy fishing pole and put Velcro tape on the fishing pole and on each paper fish.) Ask each child to share a time they felt the feeling on their fish and as a group discuss how it could feel better or suggestions on how to handle it in the future.

5. **"Apple Picking"**
   Supplies Needed: Red and green colored paper, a basket or bucket
   Instructions: Cut apple shapes out of the colored paper and write a different feeling on each apple, corresponding to a feeling discussed in the book. Place the paper apples in the basket or bucket. Ask each child to pick an apple and talk about the feeling that is on the apple. (Another option is to buy fake plastic apples and tape a paper feeling on each one.) Allow for discussion and support one another.

6. **Hot Potato**
   Supplies Needed: a small ball or a small cloth ball
   Instructions: Pass the ball around the circle and play some music. When the music stops, the child holding it must say what he/she is feeling today and why.

Self-Care Exercises

These exercises will benefit the children today and in the future.

1. **Happiness Hot Potato**
   Supplies Needed: Small Ball or Cloth Ball
   Instructions: Pass the ball around the circle and play some music. When the music stops, the child holding it must say one thing that makes them happy.

2. **Gratitude Stars**
   Supplies Needed: Yellow colored paper
   Instructions: Cut star shapes out of yellow paper and write "thank you" on one side. Have several stars available at the beginning of each class. Explain to the children that each time someone has been helpful or kind to them through actions or words, they should get a star and write the name of the helpful child on the star. This will encourage the children to help one another and help them recognize things to be grateful for.

3. **Gratitude Discussion**
   Supplies Needed: None
   Instructions: Discuss what gratitude means. Talk about when someone says "thank you" - how can you tell that they mean it? Remind the children that even on a bad day, there are things to be grateful for, such as the sun coming up or a favorite song on the radio.

4. **Affirmations**
   Supplies Needed: Large index cards; colored pencils, markers or crayons
   Instructions: Talk to the children about affirmations and how to use them. Explain how the words "I am" are so important. Use some examples that the children may have discussed during the *Feelings* portion of the class. Give them some examples if they are having difficulty creating their own affirmations. Be sure to understand affirmations yourself and how to choose appropriate words. For example, if a child has trouble keeping their room clean, suggesting *I can keep my room clean every day* as an affirmation is going to be disappointing for them if they are not able to uphold that affirmation. A better suggestion would be: *I am willing to try to keep my room clean every day.* Or *Every day, I will do my best to keep my room clean.* See Appendix J for additional resources.
   Alternate Instructions: To adapt for younger children, have the children draw a picture and decorate it. Ask the children to write "I love me" at the top of the page. Ask them to exchange the picture with someone else to keep as a gift and a reminder to love themselves.

5. **Yoga and/or Stretching**

   Supplies Needed: Knowledge of yoga postures and/or stretching techniques that kids can easily learn, yoga mats or exercise mats, or if outdoors a grassy area.

   Instructions: This may be performed indoors or outdoors. Teach the children some mindful movement exercises and/or yoga postures they can easily perform to help them find balance in their bodies, become comfortable with their breath and find stillness within. See Appendix E for Yoga Postures and Mindful Movement.

   Alternate Instructions: You can invite a qi gong instructor or yoga instructor to help teach this portion if you are not comfortable or if you don't have any experience with these forms of movement.

6. **Nature Walk**

   Supplies Needed: A nice spot outdoors

   Instructions: If you have access to a nice area outdoors, take the kids out for a stroll. Encourage them to spend time outdoors each day to recharge their energy fields. Explain the role that nature plays in our healing, from walking to simply sitting in nature for relaxation.

7. **Meditation**

   Supplies Needed: None

   Instructions: Talk to the children about meditation and how they can begin by simply focusing on their breath. You may want to set a time for 2 to 3 minutes for them to practice focusing on their breath. You can instruct them to say quietly to themselves, "I am breathing in" as they breathe in and "I am breathing out" as they breathe out. Perform a guided meditation by asking them to imagine a large waterfall of brilliant light falling down over them or guiding them to relax every muscle in their bodies starting at their feet to their head. This will give them something to focus on.

Reiki Instruction

The Reiki attunement procedure for children is the same one you learned to perform on adults. That said, there are a few things to take into consideration. As a Reiki Master Teacher, you have likely evolved your process to include how, when, and how many students per class to attune. Most often the attunement process for children is reserved for the end of the class, on or near the end of the course; it varies depending on the teacher. As you teach Reiki to children, you will learn your own preferences.

Pay close attention to the energy of the group of children you are working with; that energy will often dictate the timing and the number of children that are optimal for attunement. Personally, I've found that I never perform an attunement in the first class, but I have performed attunements in any of the following classes. Children have a much shorter attention span than adults, and particularly with younger children, it's unrealistic to expect that they'll wait quietly and patiently for very long. For this reason, I recommend attuning one child at a time and allowing the other children to do something else. Invite a parent or friend to assist you with the other children while you are performing attunements. This accomplishes two things: You will be allowed to stay in your high-frequency Reiki vibration, and the other children will be looked after. The other children can do any activity you wish; I've found that quiet activities are most valuable to you and to them. Once the children have been attuned, they tend to be more calm, balanced, and grounded and actually enjoy the quiet. Below are a few good activities for the other children to do while you are performing an attunement.

1. **Planting**
   Supplies Needed: Old newspapers, seeds, 4- to 6-inch pots, potting soil
   Instructions: Spread out newspapers on the table or floor, and have 4- to 6-inch pots available for the children to use. You can even purchase pots that they can decorate on the outside. Please see the Appendix K for some planting ideas.

2. **Draw Reiki Symbol**
   Supplies Needed: Paper; pens or pencils
   Instructions: With the children's Reiki class, I attune the children to Level One Reiki. I also teach them the Cho-Ku Rei. You can have them practice drawing the symbol.

3. **Free Arts & Crafts Time**
   Supplies Needed: Paper; crayons, pencils, or markers
   Instructions: This is an opportunity for children to draw and color whatever picture they would like. You can even assign a group project that they all work on together.

After attunement, children often seem to become more still, quiet and balanced. Once you have completed the attunement process for all children in the class, you will want to make sure that they are grounded. I particularly like the planting exercise mentioned above, because putting their hands in dirt is not only fun but also helps them to ground. You can also serve a snack to help them become more grounded.

Once the children are attuned to Reiki, it is really important to build up their self-confidence with it. There are a few ways to do this. First, be sure to give each child a certificate of completion. In Appendix L there is a sample wording for a Children's Reiki Certificate. Second - and this is the *best* way to build confidence – give the children opportunities to practice Reiki. I recommend devoting an entire class to practice. You can have them practice on each other, on their plants, or on an animal. Finally, give them an assignment to practice at home with their family members before they come back to class.

Practicing Reiki

Children can practice Reiki on:

- Each other
- Themselves
- Plants
- Pets
- Friends and family
- Meals, beverages, and snacks

Here's a great example of practicing Reiki where children can see the results. Give each child a cup filled with a carbonated beverage and have them practice Reiki on it. The Reiki energy will deflate it. It is a great visual for them to see their work. Kids love it!

Host a kid's Reiki Share. A Reiki Share is a gathering of practitioners of Reiki to support one another in their practice, develop friendships with like-minded individuals and an opportunity to give and receive Reiki treatments. They are often held monthly, and usually only for adults. This would be a unique service for children who practice Reiki, giving them not only an opportunity for Reiki practice but also a chance to build friendships and develop their intuition.

When planning to host a Reiki Share for kids, I would recommend reviewing *8 Things to Consider as You Plan Your Class* on page 1 of this book. While you can easily create Reiki Shares for specific age groups, I found that hosting Reiki Shares for children from 7 to 15 years old proved to be the most rewarding for everyone involved. Not only was it helpful for me to have the older children assist with set-up, bathroom breaks, snack time, quiet time, etc., but the care, compassion and rapport that developed amongst the various ages was extraordinary. The kids inherently "get" what adults struggle to find: the ability to understand one another, provide support to one another and be who they are without hesitation or fear of what others think. While the older kids may have adapted to societal standards of worrying about what people think, the younger kids give them permission to be who they are. The younger kids feel a sense of acceptance and belonging from their older peers, even if some of the children don't feel that way at home with their older siblings.

Overall, you will feel glad that you had the opportunity to experience the dynamics of interaction among different age groups. You will be amazed at how hopeful you become about the future of the world we live in. These kids are definitely here to make change happen, and they have what it takes to do so. We, the adults and pioneers of energy healing and understanding, are here to provide them with the support they need to embrace who they are, why they are here and how they can change things. The tools we give them today will benefit us all now and in the future. If we look to the children, not only can we learn a lot from them; we have a reason to believe there can be peace here on Earth.

A Few Final Thoughts

I hope you've found this guide to teaching children Reiki helpful and inspiring. I've included the most important things I've learned from teaching Reiki to a number of children over more than ten years. By no means must you follow the workbook in order; you may skip around to fit your own teaching plan. Below are a few general suggestions to help guide you.

Teaching Reiki should be fun for you and the children. The most important thing to remember when working with children is to make it fun and interactive. Allow yourself plenty of tools so that you don't get bored teaching the same thing over and over.

Stay flexible and alert. Your greatest gifts are your skills of intuition and observation. It is important to remain as flexible as you can. Sometimes your lessons may go as planned; other times you'll find that you haven't accomplished what you hoped to because other things needed your attention. That's okay! By staying alert to the classroom conditions and changing directions when necessary, you can still achieve your overall goals for the course. The more you teach children, the more comfortable you will become.

Have a plan and think about the big picture. My general rule of thumb is that I have a plan about what I would like to accomplish by the end of the course, but it doesn't matter to me how I get there—as long as those things are covered. As you begin working with children, your intuition will kick in and you will discover which exercises help which age group. You will discover lots of things on your own too!

Take care of you. We've all heard the saying about putting on your own "oxygen mask" first. This is as true for Reiki teachers as for any other teacher or caregiver, if not more so. You can't effectively share the joy of Reiki if you are not taking care of yourself. Working on yourself and using the tools you have as a healer is really important. I've included several helpful documents in the Appendices at the end of this book. Use them to keep your teaching fresh and keep yourself inspired.

Appendix A

The Benefits of Children Learning Reiki

Reiki, an ancient Japanese healing technique, is used for promoting relaxation and stress reduction and physical, mental and emotional healing. We are all made up of energy; Reiki will teach your child about their energy and connection to every living thing. It will provide your child with a way to give comforting, loving energy to themselves as well as to other living beings, such as to their pets and special people in their life. Along with this, Reiki will:

Provide a greater sense of self-esteem:

- Empower your child to make their own decisions and stand up for what they believe.
- Help your child accept themselves as they are; bringing more balance into their life.
- Help your child discover their inherent intuition and how it can benefit them in their life.

Raise their self-awareness:

- Equip your child with an understanding of their interaction with the environment they are in.
- Enable your child to identify and understand their emotions while learning new ways to channel "negative" emotions.
- Encourage better choices for their well-being such as eating healthier, exercising and understanding how their physical bodies react to stress.

Promote relaxation:

- Teach your child how to handle anxiety in a healthy way.
- Help your child reach and maintain a calmer state of mind when they are feeling pressured.
- Improve your child's sleep patterns, focus and concentration.
- Help your child to develop and achieve their goals.

With the knowledge of Reiki, children become empowered and self-aware, making their world a better place and effectively changing our world as well. Some practical benefits to the community are:

- Decreases aggressive and violent behavior at home and in schools, e.g., bullying.
- Builds stronger resistance to peer pressure regarding destructive behaviors.
- Increases interest in establishing peace in and around their community.
- Builds awareness of their connection to all living things: people, plants, animals and the Earth.

Our children are the future; why not provide them with a tool that will make their experience of growing up more magnificent? Reiki will provide them with the right forum for manifesting a life of love, peace and harmony.

Appendix B

Children's Reiki Class Registration Form

Date of the Class: _____ - _____

Child's Full Name: _____

Date of Birth: _____

Parent/Guardian's Name: _____

Parent /Guardian's Mobile Number: _____

Address: _____

City: _____ State: _____ Zip: _____

Parent/Guardian's Email: _____

Does your child have any food allergies or special needs? _____

If yes, please specify: _____

_____

_____

_____

Who will be dropping off or picking up your child on the day(s) of the class?

_____

_____

I hereby give permission for my child _____ to attend the Children's
Reiki Class.

_____   _____

Parent/Guardian's Signature   Date

Appendix C

Children's Reiki Class Outline

Below is a suggested outline for a class of four to six students, taught over six weeks for 90 minute sessions. Remember to begin each session with an Ice Breaker/Socialization/Connection Exercise and a reminder of the rules, and provide opportunities for movement and a snack.

Class One

Begin class with music and movement to bring clarity and focus. Teach a grounding technique.

Create and play with an energy ball. Practice playing with energy. Create a pendulum to feel energy. Talk about feeling energy.

Class Two

Talk about auras. Practice seeing and drawing each other's auras. Assign children to practice viewing auras at home. Use the *Arms Wide* aura exercise. If there's extra time, start chakras.

Class Three

Talk about chakras. Talk about the colors associated with them. Do an exercise to connect the auras to their colors

Talk about feelings. Select two to talk about that day and have the children draw pictures and talk about what each one feels like. Identify feelings in the body. Ask them to go home and work on identifying their feelings until you see each other again.

Class Four

Discuss feelings again. Talk about different ways we can cope with feelings. Each child should have an opportunity to explore feelings during class. Use mindful movement such as stretching or yoga.

Discuss the six senses. Explore each sense and talk about how our intuitive sense functions. Guided imagery/meditation.

Class Five

Talk about how we show love to ourselves. Discuss self-care, including healthy eating, a good night's sleep, drinking plenty of water and always communicating feelings.

Class Six

Perform Reiki attunement on the students. Practice Reiki on each other.

Appendix D

Snack Recipes

Blueberry Gummy Bears
Makes 30-40 Gummies depending on the size of the molds, enough for 7-10 kids
Ingredients:
- 1 cup blueberries (frozen wild blueberries work well here)
- 1/2 cup lemon juice (from about 4 lemons)
- 1/2 cup coconut manna or raw coconut spread (e.g. Nature's Way or Nutiva brands)
- 2 tbsp maple syrup (or another sweetener)
- 4 tbsp beef gelatin (Great Lakes brand)

Preparation
1. In a small saucepan over low heat, bring the first four ingredients to a gentle boil. Remove from the heat and stir until the coconut is melted and well combined. Put the gelatin powder into a blender and add the warm blueberry mixture. Process until completely smooth (the mixture will be fairly thick).

2. Pour the mixture into candy molds (I have a gummy bear mold!) or an 8- by 8-inch glass dish lined on the bottom with parchment paper. Refrigerate for 2 hours.

3. When the mixture is set, gently tease the contents out of the candy mold, if using, or out of the glass dish and onto a chopping board. If you didn't use a candy mold, cut the gummy mixture into bite-sized pieces, using a cookie cutter to make shapes if you wish. Store in the refrigerator for up to 5 days.

Kale Chips
Makes enough for 4 kids
Ingredients
- 1 large bunch kale (can use purple or curly)
- 2 tablespoons olive oil (or more enough to coat kale)
- 1/4 - 1/2 teaspoon salt
- 1-2 teaspoons of nutritional yeast

Preparation
1. Preheat the oven to 350°F. Remove and discard the center rib and stems from each kale leaf. Tear or cut the leaves into bite-size pieces, about 2 to 3 inches wide. Wash the kale and dry it very well.
2. Place the kale in a large bowl. Drizzle with the oil and sprinkle with the salt and nutritional yeast. Massage the oil and seasonings into the kale with your hands to distribute evenly. Place the kale in a single layer on 3 baking sheets, and bake until crisp and the edges are slightly browned, 12 to 15 minutes.

Healthy Chocolate Pudding

Makes 4 1/2-cup servings

Ingredients

- 2 medium size (very ripe) avocados
- 1/4 - 1/3 cup maple syrup or agave nectar
- 2 tsp extra virgin coconut oil (melt at a LOW temp to turn to liquid)
- 1 tsp vanilla extract
- Pinch of sea salt
- 4 Tbsp raw cacao (cocoa) powder
- 1/4 cup of water (might need to adjust slightly)
- 1 cup fresh berries

Preparation

Put all ingredients into a food processor or high-speed blender; blend until smooth. Adjust to taste. Transfer to individual bowls and refrigerator until ready to serve. Garnish with berries.

Recipe: Vanilla & Honey Avocado Pudding

Makes 2 1/2-cup servings

Ingredients

- 1 ripe medium size avocado
- 2 to 3 Tbsp raw honey or agave nectar (adjust to taste)
- 2 tsp vanilla extract
- 1 tsp chia seeds
- 1 c almond, coconut, or cashew milk

Preparation

1. Place the avocado, honey or agave nectar, vanilla extract and chia seeds in a blender or food processor. While blending, slowly pour in the nut milk until the pudding reaches a creamy consistency.

2. Divide among ramekins or glasses and refrigerate at least 30 minutes.

3. Top with sliced almonds and serve.

Peanut Butter Chocolate Chip Cookie Dough Bites

Makes 14 cookies

Ingredients

- 1 1/4 c canned chickpeas, well-rinsed and patted dry with a paper towel
- 2 tsp vanilla extract
- 1/2 c + 2 Tbsp natural peanut butter, SunButter Natural or almond butter - room temperature
- 1/4 c honey, agave or maple syrup
- 1 tsp baking powder
- Pinch of sea salt (if nut butter is unsalted)
- 1/2 c chocolate chips (use vegan and dairy-free chocolate chips, if needed)

Preparation

1. Preheat your oven to 350°F / 175°C. Combine all the ingredients, except for the chocolate chips, in a food processor and process until very smooth. Make sure to scrape the sides and the top to get the little chunks of chickpeas and process again until they're combined.

2. Put in the chocolate chips and stir it if you can, or pulse it once or twice. The mixture will be very thick and sticky.

3. With wet hands, form into 1 1/2" balls. Place onto a Silpat or a piece of parchment paper. If you want them to look more like normal cookies, press down slightly on the balls. They don't do much rising.

4. Bake for about 10 minutes. The dough balls will still be very soft when you take them out of the oven. They will not set like normal cookies.

5. Store in an airtight container at room temperature (or in the fridge) for up to 1 week.

Appendix E

Movement Resources

There are several good reasons to adding movement to your class, as I've noted throughout this manual. Personally, I find the most important reasons are that it's a fun way to teach children to be healthy, to develop body awareness and to become more present with themselves. For the purpose of this class, I have suggested three forms of body expression through movement: dancing, mindful movement and yoga. All three of these provide movement opportunities suitable for children of all ages, sizes and varying degrees of physical abilities; they can be modified as needed.

It is important to know your audience and their capabilities as well as knowing your own too. If dancing isn't your thing, there is always qi qong, yoga or mindful movement. When a particular form of movement would be beneficial, I've suggested it throughout this manual, but feel free to change it up depending on your goals. The key is to make movement as fun as possible so that children stay engaged. If most of the children are following along, you're doing great. If not, it's time to change it up a bit and move on to a different exercise.

Dancing

I've always used free dancing at the beginning of my classes, for both adults and children. It helps release the energy students bring with them to class. This idea came to me when my five-year-old niece spent the weekend with me. Even at the tender age of 5, she was experiencing a lot of stress and unhealthy behaviors due to her parents' divorce. I felt I needed a way to help her free herself from all the stress and emotion she was carrying, and I recalled how freeing dancing always felt to me, so I included it in the first 15 to 30 minutes of our visit together. I simply turned up the music and started to move freely in whatever way felt good.

This particular movement exercise can be guided or unstructured. This is best determined by the age group, ability and response of the children to this exercise. If the children jump right in and start dancing, let them go at it in their own unique way. If you find they are not moving or uncertain how to move, you may want to shout out directions, for example, *Move your hips, Shake your hands, Shrug your shoulders,* etc. Another option would be to use music that guides you to do some body movements, such as the song *I Pull it Down from the Heavens* from Mark Stanton Welch's CD *Dance Your Spirit* or the song *Over There* from Mark Stanton Welch's CD *Trust Your Vibes.* The songs don't tell you what to do, but it's easy to direct the children with the words. And don't forget: Often children will only participate if you dance too!

Children's Yoga

Yoga has become a more accepted form of movement for children in the last several years due to its many physical benefits. Yoga builds balance and flexibility, strengthens motor coordination and develops muscle tone. It is also extremely complementary to Reiki. Energy (including Reiki energy) can become stagnant and stuck in the body, but yoga helps it circulate throughout the body. Because Reiki energy healing is so high-vibration, it has a tendency to un-ground children; yoga can help children ground and anchor themselves in their physical bodies after performing Reiki.

There are many books, videos and teachers that can help you with yoga postures for children, but to get you started I'm sharing some of my favorites below. The primary reason for teaching yoga postures to Reiki students is to help them enhance their Reiki practice and instill good self-care. I recommend teaching only three to five yoga postures, holding each for 10 to 20 seconds or longer. Use your judgment when determining which and how many postures to teach based on the age group and ability of the class. Keep in mind that this is an opportunity for children to explore how yoga feels in their body, and allow them to practice at their own pace and according to their abilities. Begin to create a pattern of breathing with the children prior to starting the exercises below, and then encourage them to maintain good breathing habits throughout the postures.

Yoga Postures

1. **Standing/Mountain Posture**
   Instructions: Stand upright with your feet and toes together, and choose a spot directly in front of you to look at. Do a shoulder shrug, bringing your shoulders up and then back down. Remember to breathe in and out fully! While this exercise sounds simple, it activates several muscles in your body and encourages good posture, balance and grounding.

2. **Tree Posture**
   Instructions: Stand straight and focus your eyes on a spot on the wall in front of you. Shift your weight from both legs to your left leg and foot. Then bend and lift your right leg up off the ground, turning it out to the side (your right knee will point out to the right). Now pull your right foot up and place it on your left inner thigh or calf, whichever is most comfortable for you. Can you balance in this position? If so, place your hands in prayer position over your chest, then reach your arms up above your head, keeping them in prayer position. Hold, then release the posture and come back to center with your feet together and your weight evenly distributed. Now let's repeat the post with your other

leg. Don't forget to breathe in and out fully! The tree posture encourage good balance and awareness of your core muscles, and it also strengthens the legs.

3. **The Triangle**

    Instructions: Stand with your legs spread apart and your feet out past your hips. Raise your arms out to the sides so that you're stretching out horizontally. Keep your arms and legs straight and bend to the left, placing your left hand on your left calf or thigh while your right arm reaches up toward the sky. Is this posture comfortable for you? If so, look up toward your right hand. Hold, then release the pose and come back to center with your feet together. Now let's repeat the pose on the opposite side. Don't forget to breathe in and out fully! The triangle pose encourages good balance, strengthens your hips and legs, and opens your heart.

4. **Cow and Cat Posture**

    Instructions: Kneel on all fours with your hands and knees on the floor. Your back should be in a neutral, flat position. Let your belly sink, then curl your tailbone up and lift your head to look toward the sky. (This is the cow posture.) Okay, now pull your belly up and in, and curl your spine so that your neck almost touches your chest. (This is the cat posture.) Now slowly alternate between the cow and the cat posture, five times. Breathe in as your head goes up; breathe out as your head goes down. This cow and the cat are great for spine health; they make you more flexible and help your energy flow.

5. **Downward Dog/Upside Down "V" Posture**

    Instructions: Kneel on all fours with your hands and knees on the floor. Your back should be in a neutral, flat position. Lift your tailbone high up in the air like a dog or cat does when it's stretching. Push your shoulders back and start to "unbend" your legs into a standing position, dropping your head down toward your knees. Your legs and arms will go straight into an upside down "V." Don't forget to breathe in and out! The downward dog posture calms your brain, releases stress and stretches your legs, arms and hands.

6. **Sitting Posture**

    Instructions: Kneel on your knees, then sit back on top of your feet with your spine straight. Focus on the wall in front of you, and breathe in 6 full, deep breaths.

7. **Child's Posture**

    Instructions: From the *Sitting Posture*, stretch your arms out in front of you and bend forward at your hips. If it's comfortable for you, keep bending until your forehead touches the floor in front of you. Bring your arms back by your sides, and breath in and out fully! You can use a pillow under your forehead if it's more comfortable.

Mindful Movement

The following exercises are a great way to incorporate movement into your class without requiring too much time. Stretching is a key component in maintaining auric body (energy body) health. I really like these exercises because they not only meet the need for some movement but also help children rebalance their emotions, energies and thoughts and bring them into alignment with their well-being. It also gives them an opportunity to learn to move their bodies more consciously and in a different way than they may be used to. Mindful movement is a great addition to children's Reiki healing "toolbox" and it can also enhance their self-care routine. I use techniques with my adult classes in my children's classes. The descriptions below are adapted from Donna Eden's book *Energy Medicine*.

1. **Heaven Rushing In** (*about 2 minutes*) Helps children bring themselves into the present.
   - Stand tall. Take a moment to ground yourself by spreading your fingers on your thighs, breathe in deeply, feel your feet on the ground, and become conscious of the Earth beneath you. Imagine that the energy from your fingers is pouring down your thighs and into the ground.
   - Take a deep breath in, open your arms wide and bring them into a prayer position in front of your chest. Now breathe out.
   - Take another deep breath, open your arms wide, and lift them. Look up to heaven (the sky or the ceiling). Reach toward heaven, then release your breath. Your hands may feel tingly or warm.
   - Wait for your hands to feel a sensation, then scoop that energy into your arms and bring it into your heart center. Allow your hands to send this energy into your body through your heart.
   - If you want to send it to a specific part of your body, you can do that instead.

2. **The Cross Crawl** (*about 3 minutes*) Balances left and right brain, improves coordination.
   - Start in a standing position and lift your right arm while lifting your left leg at the same time.
   - Now, as you lower your right arm and left leg, raise your left arm and right leg. Now let's repeat from the beginning, but this time lift your leg more and swing your arm across the middle of your body to the opposite side of your body.
   - Continue this exaggerated "march" for at least 1 to 2 minutes, breathing deeply through your nose and out through your mouth.
   - *Alternative:* Have the children march exaggeratedly around the room. *If someone is not able to stand, they can perform these exercises in a chair.*

3. **Connecting Heaven and Earth** *(about 2 minutes)* Releases excess energy.

- Rub your hands together, shake them off and place them on your thighs with your fingers spread.
- Take a deep breath in and circle your arms out to your sides.
- As you exhale, bring your hands into prayer position in front of your heart chakra.
- Take another deep breath, step out to the right, and stretch your right hand up and out to the right with your palm facing up like you're pushing something above you. Now look up toward the heavens. Stretch your other arm down and out to the left with your palm facing down like you're pushing something into the earth. Stay in this position for as long as you can hold the breath.
- Now release your breath through your mouth and return your hands to prayer position in front of your chest. Repeat on the other side. Then do two more sets.
- Coming out of the pose, drop your arms down and bend at your waist. Let your arms hang there with your knees slightly bent, and take two deep breaths. Slowly return to a standing position and roll your shoulders back.

Appendix F

Music Resources

Shaina Knoll, *Songs for the Inner Child.* https://www.shainanoll.com/

Mark Stanton Welch, *Trust Your Vibes. Dance Your Spirit. Chants.*
http://musicforeverysoul.com/index.html

Mike Rowland, *The Fairy Ring.*

If you choose to do mindful movement and/or yoga with children, you can find many other resources through an online search.

Appendix G

Angel Prayer

This simple Angel Prayer is suitable for many different occasions. I say it every night before going to bed. Children can use it before bed or when they are scared, as well as when they are preparing for Reiki. It provides a sense of comfort knowing that unseen helpers are always here with us.

May Michael be at my right hand,

Gabriel at my left,

Before me Uriel,

Behind me Raphael,

And above my head

The divine presence of God.

Appendix H

Children's Grounding Meditation

To purchase a recording of this meditation, please contact me at april@soulstarhealing.com.

Appendix I

Feelings Resources

Within my first few classes teaching Reiki to children, I learned that a discussion about feelings is important. Through simple conversation, I learned that not only do many children *not* understand their feelings, but the ones who *do* are often on the cusp of learning to squash them down. Suppressing our feelings is one of the biggest ways we begin to wear down our energy fields and cause dis-ease within our physical bodies. My early conversations with children in class made it clear that I needed to start addressing feelings in a kid-friendly way. Once I realized this, it gave me a great deal of enthusiasm and inspiration to work new material into my classes. It intuitively felt *right* to incorporate feelings into children's Reiki instruction.

There are various books about how to talk with children about their emotions. On the pages that follow, you'll find a short list of books I have used along the way to get the conversation started. But first, here are some points on how to begin.

> 1. Everyone feels emotions! Children feel the same emotions as adults, but they may not express them the same way. Oftentimes, kids have a difficult time understanding their feelings and struggle to express them; this may cause them to shut down and develop negative coping skills.

> 2. Identify feelings--open a new vocabulary! We have been given a rainbow of emotions, not just happy and sad. There are many words to identify how we may be feeling, and as human beings we are fortunate to experience them all. Talk about different words children can use to describe their emotions. I chose *confused, mad,* and *embarrassed* as well as *happy* and *silly* because they seemed to be the ones most needed.

> 3. Help children understand *why* they need to know about feelings! Identifying emotions is the first step to discovering how to express yourself and what you're experiencing. It provides a better insight into your life experience. I often describe emotions as being like a compass. Emotions are the way we navigate through life. If you can identify an unpleasant feeling, you can look for a way to change the situation that's causing it or you can learn how to cope with it in a healthier way.

4. Listen to each other! After the first week of discussion around feelings, make tuning in to feelings a part of your class each week. Weekly check-ins and short discussions are crucial to helping children develop a sense of ease around their feelings. It provides them with a safe realm to discuss how they feel without repercussions. As you have these discussions, be sure not to deny how a child may be feeling or minimize what a child is feeling, even you find it uncomfortable. For example: a child may say, "I don't like school." You might ask, "what don't you like about school?" and allow them to answer without judgment. The key is to listen, acknowledge and respect what each child may be feeling.

5. Lead by example! Participate in feelings activities with the children and share how you feel. Be mindful of your audience, however; don't share too much. For example, you might say, "I feel tired." A child might ask you why. Your could respond, "I didn't sleep very well last night." You don't have to give a long story, just enough context to show the children that it 's healthy to express their feelings and to model talking about feelings.

6. Explain how feelings and intuition work together. Feelings are one way we can recognize our intuition. If we know what we are feeling then we can easily identify when it is our feeling versus someone else's. This is a good time to explain how we take on other people's energy in our auras through interaction. It also helps us to understand empathy better, which leads to understanding someone else better.

I could write pages and pages about feelings and still feel as if I haven't said enough. But the best thing I can say to you is to allow your own intuition to be the guide. When I started teaching, I often looked for a poem or a child's book to get the discussion started, but after a while I allowed myself to be guided by the children's energy when they came to class. Once you become comfortable teaching children and allowing your intuition to kick in, you, too, may let go of the resources and dive in with your own ideas. Just be sure to mentally prepare yourself for discussing feelings; the conversation tends to takes on a life of its own.

Below are some of the resources I used to start a discussion around feelings.

Silverstein, Shel, "Whatif." *A Light in the Attic*. New York: Harper & Row, Publisher's Inc. 1981. Page 90. Print.

Loomans, Diane with Julia Loomans. *100 Ways to Build Self-Esteem and Teach Values*. New York: HJ Kramer, Inc. 1994. Print.

Godwin, Patricia. *I Feel Orange Today*. Toronto, Canada: Annick Press. 2000. Print.

Madison, Lynda, Dr. *The Feelings Book: The Care and Keeping of Your Emotions*. Middleton, Wisconsin: Pleasant Company Publications. 2002. Print.

Curtis, Jamie Lee. *Today I Feel Silly and Other Moods That Make My Day*. USA: Harper Children. 1998. Print.

Appendix J

Understanding "I Am" & Affirmations

The words "I am" are the two most powerful words in the English language. In every language on the planet, you will find the words "I am." These two words put the command behind what you say and create the reality you live in. Any words you place after the words "I am" create your experience. For example: "I am tired" keeps you literally in the cycle of being tired. Instead, say "I feel tired." A feeling will pass, whereas "I am" is a state of being that creates more tiredness.

Likewise, every affirmation begins with "I am." An affirmation places your intention actively in the first person, as if you have already achieved it. For example: "I will heal" tells the world that you will heal at some point in the future, but "I am healed" says that the healing has already happened. "I am" is powerful: it can keep you stuck in a bad place or move you toward your dreams.

For a deeper understanding of "I am," I suggest reading the books for adults listed below. (A side note: *The Power of Intention* and *Excuse Me, Your Life is Waiting* are the two books that have had the most influence on my life. They prompted me to start my business.)

Below are some resources for you to use in learning the understanding of "I am" and affirmations.

<u>Adult Reading</u>

Dyer, Wayne. *The Power of Intention*. USA: Hay House Inc. 2004. Print

Dyer, Wayne. *Wishes Fulfilled: Mastering the Art of Manifesting*. USA: Hay House Inc. 2013. Print

Grabhorn, Lynn. *Excuse Me, Your Life is Waiting*. USA. Hampton Roads Publishing; 15th Printing Edition. 2003.

<u>Children's Reading</u>

Dyer, Wayne. *I Am: How Two Little Words Mean So Much*. USA: Hay House Inc. 2012. Print

Dyer, Wayne. *Incredible You: 10 Ways to Let Your Greatness Shine Through*. USA: Hay House Inc. 2005. Print

Dyer, Wayne. *No Excuses!: How What You Say Can Get In Your Way*. USA: Hay House Inc. 2009. Print

Dyer, Wayne. *Unstoppable Me: 10 Ways to Soar Through Life*. USA: Hay House Inc. 2006. Print

Hay, Louis L. and Kristina Tracy. *I Think, I Am: Teaching Kids the Power of Affirmations.* USA. Hay House Inc. 2008 Print.

Meador, Celine Wood. *Dream Big, By Durn!* Charlotte, North Carolina. ARC Publications. 1995. Print.

Appendix K:

Planting Resources

The idea of planting with children during a Reiki class came from the realization that Reiki is in everything, including plants. This activity gives children the opportunity to learn responsibility and caretaking as they plant each seed and nurture it with water and sunlight as it grows. They'll also learn that performing Reiki helps plants grow and flourish more quickly.

Over the years, I have altered this activity to fit the needs of the time, the age of children I was working with and the availability of the seeds. I didn't really have a plan on how I would accomplish this activity when I first started, so there was a lot of trial and error. At first, I bought little plants already blooming for my students to perform Reiki on, but what I found was that some plants don't stay blooming for too long and the children thought the plants had died. Then I decided to start planting from scratch; I thought I'd just pick up pots, potting soil and seeds at a local store to use. That wasn't quite successful, so I reached out to a friend, Master Gardener Patricia Laudano, for advice. With her help, I've put together an easier, more effective plan that may help you too.

3 Things to Consider when Deciding What to Plant

1. Choose a pot. There are a couple options. Why not choose:
    - Biodegradable pots - they're great for the environment
    - Decorate-able pots - so kids can create their own beautiful planters

2. Choose what to plant. Here are a couple of simple rules for when you're starting to grow plants indoors: *If the seed is fairly large, it will germinate quicker and grow faster. Use 2 seeds per pot.*
    - Beans, corn, pumpkin seeds, peas, zucchini and avocado seeds are nice, large choices for growing produce.
    - You can also place cut vegetable parts in water and watch them sprout roots, leaves or more of the vegetable. Try celery, carrot tops, sweet potatoes, scallions or radish tops.
    - Sunflower seeds are the by far the largest and best flower seeds to grow indoors with kids.
    - Marigolds and zinnias are good, smaller seeds for germinating flowers more quickly.

3. Choose your soil.
    - Buy organic! It is safe and non-toxic for children and the Earth.
    - Buy **WONDER SOIL**®. It is a lightweight, soil-less growing medium made from Premium Coco Coir. It promotes a stronger root system, faster germination and enhanced plant growth.

Now that you know what to plant and you have your supplies, it is time to carry out the activity itself. Cover your work area with a newspaper or tablecloth for easy cleanup. Warn the parents and/or guardians ahead of time so they can dress children in clothes they don't mind soiling. If the children will be decorating their own pots, allow one day for decorating and one for planting. Below are some suggestions on how to incorporate the planting exercise into your schedule.

1. **Day of Attunement.** If you have pots for children to decorate, they can spend their time decorating pots while someone is receiving their attunement. When the attunements are finished, if there's time, you can fill up the pots with soil and plant seeds. Give each child a wooden craft stick and write their name and date on one side and the type of vegetable or fruit on the other side. Send each child home with their planted pot; ask them to perform Reiki on it daily and bring it back to class next week to discuss its progress.

2. **Day Other than Attunement.** If you're not doing attunements and the children will be decorating their own pots, it's best to separate the decorating and planting into two different classes. When it's time to do the planting, have them fill each pot with soil and plant a seed. Give each child a wooden craft stick and write their name and date on one side and the type of vegetable or fruit on the other side. You can either send them home with the plant and tell them to bring it back on attunement day or you can keep the plants in class hand until then. If you choose the latter, every week have your students water and talk to their plant. (This is an ideal opportunity to discuss affirmations and how talking nicely to plants helps them grow.) On Reiki attunement day, send each child home with their plant and tell them to perform Reiki on it daily. Ask them to bring it back to class the following week to discuss its progress.

3. **Last day of class.** When it is time to do the planting, have each child fill a pot with soil and plant a seed. Give each child a wooden craft stick and write their name and date on one side and the type of vegetable or fruit on the other side. Send each child home with their plant and ask them to perform Reiki on it daily. Ask them to bring it back when they come for a Reiki Share to report on its growth.

Appendix L

Sample Children's Reiki Certificate

This is to certify that

On this day, (date of final class)

Child's Full Name

Participated in the Kid's Reiki Program, in which

he/she has received the Level One Attunement

of Usui Reiki Empowerment.

Your Signature

Printed: Your Name, Title: Reiki Master Teacher

Printed: Business Name, Address, Contact Info